PANCREATITIS DIET COOKBOOK 2025

The Easy Delicious Recipes including Full Color Images, Meal Plan, Health Benefits and More

FRANK J. WESTON

Frank J. Weston

Copyright © 2025 by Frank J. Weston

All rights reserved. No part of this publication may be reproduced, distributed, or transmitted in any form or by any means, including photocopying, recording, or other electronic or mechanical methods, without the prior written permission of the publisher, except in the case of brief quotations embodied in critical reviews and certain other noncommercial uses permitted by copyright law.

Published By Frank J. Weston

Table of Contents

Introduction 5
   Understanding Pancreatitis and Its Impact 5
   The Role of Nutrition in Healing 6
   Key Nutrients for Pancreatic Health 6
   Foods to Embrace and Avoid 8

Stocking Your Pancreatitis Friendly Kitchen 10
   Friendly Pantry Essentials 11
   Low-Fat Cooking Staples 12
   Tools and Tips for Simplified Cooking 13
   Meal Prep Techniques to Save Time 14

Nourishing Breakfasts to Kickstart Healing 16
   Introduction to Nourishing Breakfast 17

Light and Satisfying Lunches 26

Wholesome Snacks for Pancreatic Relief 36

Low-Fat Main Courses 46

Easy, Soothing Soups 56

Fiber-Rich Dinners for Digestive Support 66

Comforting Desserts and Treats 76

7-Day Meal Plan for Lasting Pancreatic Health 86

Conclusion 90

Introduction
Understanding Pancreatitis and Its Impact

Pancreatitis is an inflammatory condition of the pancreas, a small but crucial organ located behind the stomach. The pancreas plays a dual role in both digestion and regulating blood sugar by producing enzymes and hormones, including insulin. When pancreatitis occurs, the pancreas becomes inflamed, often leading to serious abdominal pain, nausea, vomiting, and other symptoms. The inflammation can be acute, occurring suddenly and lasting a few days, or chronic, which lasts over years and can progressively worse, damaging the pancreas permanently.

The impact of pancreatitis goes beyond immediate discomfort. Over time, chronic pancreatitis can impair the pancreas' ability to produce essential enzymes that break down fats and proteins in the diet, resulting in malnutrition. In severe cases, it may lead to complications such as diabetes, digestive issues, and even pancreatic cancer. This makes managing the condition not only a priority for immediate relief but a long-term health imperative.

What many people may not realize is that pancreatitis is closely linked to dietary habits. Poor food choices, such as a high intake of alcohol, processed foods, and saturated fats, often trigger or exacerbate the inflammation. Consequently, individuals diagnosed with pancreatitis must make significant adjustments to their eating patterns to both reduce flare-ups and promote healing.

Understanding how diet affects pancreatitis is the first step in making conscious, informed decisions about what to eat. Not only does it allow for better symptom management, but it also empowers those affected to take an active role in their healing journey. Diet becomes more than just fuel; it becomes a therapeutic tool that can help support the pancreas and overall digestive health.

The Role of Nutrition in Healing

When managing pancreatitis, nutrition becomes the cornerstone of treatment and recovery. The connection between diet and inflammation is undeniable, especially when it comes to a sensitive organ like the pancreas. Nutrition serves multiple purposes in healing pancreatitis: reducing inflammation, supporting digestion, preventing malnutrition, and avoiding the recurrence of symptoms.

First, a well-managed diet can dramatically reduce the inflammation of the pancreas. By consuming anti-inflammatory foods, like leafy greens, berries, and lean proteins, the body can better cope with the stress placed on the pancreas. These foods are packed with antioxidants, which help to neutralize harmful free radicals that can contribute to cellular damage and inflammation.

Second, proper nutrition aids in the digestion of food, particularly when the pancreas isn't functioning optimally. Since the pancreas is responsible for producing enzymes that break down fats, carbohydrates, and proteins, individuals with pancreatitis may struggle with digesting these nutrients. Low-fat, easy-to-digest foods, such as steamed vegetables, lean meats, and low-fat dairy, can lighten the load on the pancreas and prevent malabsorption issues.

Malnutrition is another critical concern for those suffering from chronic pancreatitis. Because the pancreas can no longer produce the necessary enzymes in adequate amounts, many nutrients from food may not be absorbed properly, leading to deficiencies. Diets rich in essential vitamins and minerals—such as calcium, iron, and fat-soluble vitamins (A, D, E, and K)—become crucial to offset the impact of malnutrition. Incorporating these nutrients, along with pancreatic enzyme supplements (as prescribed by a healthcare provider), can significantly improve nutritional intake and overall well-being.

Additionally, nutrition helps prevent further damage to the pancreas by encouraging healthy weight maintenance and reducing fat intake. Being overweight or consuming high-fat meals can trigger acute pancreatitis flare-ups, so a diet centered on moderate portions, healthy fats, and high-fiber foods can keep the pancreas from becoming overburdened.

Perhaps the most critical aspect of nutrition in healing is that it supports long-term pancreatic health. By establishing sustainable eating habits focused on whole, unprocessed foods, individuals can actively reduce the risk of future flare-ups and live more comfortably. Nutrition becomes an ongoing strategy, not just for managing symptoms but for thriving despite the condition.

Key Nutrients for Pancreatic Health

For individuals living with pancreatitis, choosing the right nutrients can significantly influence their overall health and quality of life. Certain nutrients play a pivotal role in reducing inflammation, supporting digestion, and promoting the healing of the pancreas. Including these nutrients in the diet ensures that the body receives what it needs without further straining the pancreas.

- **Antioxidants:** Foods rich in antioxidants, such as berries, leafy greens, and colorful vegetables, are essential in fighting inflammation and oxidative stress in the body. Antioxidants protect pancreatic cells from further damage caused by free radicals, which are unstable molecules that can exacerbate inflammation. These foods can help calm the inflammation that contributes to the onset of pancreatitis.
- **Lean Proteins:** Protein is essential for tissue repair and overall body function, but for individuals with pancreatitis, it's crucial to focus on lean protein sources. Fatty proteins, such as red meat and processed meats, can worsen symptoms, while lean options, like chicken breast, turkey, fish, and plant-based proteins (such as lentils and tofu), provide the necessary nutrients without taxing the pancreas. Protein shakes formulated specifically for pancreatitis patients can also provide an easy-to-digest alternative.
- **Low-Fat Dairy:** High-fat dairy products can trigger pancreatitis symptoms, so switching to low-fat or non-fat options is highly recommended. Low-fat yogurt, skim milk, and low-fat cheese are excellent alternatives that allow patients to continue enjoying dairy without risking further inflammation. Additionally, fortified dairy products provide calcium and vitamin D, essential for bone health, particularly when pancreatitis affects the absorption of these nutrients.
- **Healthy Fats:** While fat intake must be controlled, certain healthy fats, such as those found in avocados, olive oil, and fatty fish, provide essential omega-3 fatty acids that help reduce inflammation. These fats, in moderation, can be beneficial for overall health and should replace saturated fats, which can exacerbate pancreatitis.
- **Whole Grains:** Whole grains such as brown rice, quinoa, oatmeal, and whole wheat bread are rich in fiber and help promote good digestion. These grains help stabilize blood sugar levels and provide a steady release of energy, which is particularly important for those with pancreatitis who might experience digestive difficulties.
- **Hydration:** Staying hydrated is crucial for digestive health and overall well-being. Individuals with pancreatitis should prioritize water and herbal teas while avoiding sugary or carbonated beverages that can irritate the digestive system. Proper hydration supports enzyme function and helps the pancreas perform its role in digestion more effectively.
- **Fat-Soluble Vitamins:** People with pancreatitis often have difficulty absorbing fat-soluble vitamins like A, D, E, and K. Incorporating foods rich in these vitamins, or taking supplements as advised by a healthcare provider, is vital for maintaining eye health, immune function, bone density, and skin health. Including leafy greens, carrots, fortified dairy,

and fish can help maintain proper vitamin levels.

By focusing on these key nutrients, individuals can support their pancreas, reduce inflammation, and improve their overall health. The right balance of nutrients can make a significant difference in managing symptoms and preventing flare-ups.

Foods to Embrace and Avoid

Foods to Embrace:

- **Fruits and Vegetables:** Fresh fruits and vegetables are the cornerstone of a pancreatitis-friendly diet. These nutrient-dense foods are packed with vitamins, minerals, and antioxidants that support healing and reduce inflammation. Vegetables such as spinach, kale, broccoli, and carrots are especially beneficial. Opt for fresh or frozen varieties without added sugars or sauces.
- **Lean Proteins:** As mentioned earlier, lean proteins such as skinless poultry, fish, and tofu are great options for maintaining muscle mass and providing essential nutrients without excess fat. Fish like salmon and mackerel also offer omega-3 fatty acids, which have anti-inflammatory properties that benefit the pancreas.
- **Whole Grains:** Complex carbohydrates found in whole grains provide lasting energy and are gentle on the pancreas. Foods like oatmeal, brown rice, and quinoa are excellent sources of fiber, which aids in digestion and helps stabilize blood sugar levels.
- **Low-Fat Dairy:** Low-fat or fat-free dairy products can be enjoyed by individuals with pancreatitis without causing flare-ups. Skim milk, low-fat yogurt, and reduced-fat cheese can provide essential nutrients like calcium without overloading the pancreas with fats.
- **Healthy Fats:** While a low-fat diet is critical, small amounts of healthy fats are important for overall health. Avocados, nuts (in small portions), and olive oil are excellent choices when consumed in moderation. These fats are easier to digest and provide necessary nutrients.

Foods to Avoid:

- **High-Fat Foods:** Foods rich in saturated fats, such as fried foods, fast food, and high-fat dairy products (butter, cream, whole milk), can trigger pancreatitis symptoms. These foods are difficult to digest and increase inflammation, placing undue stress on the pancreas.
- **Processed and Sugary Foods:** Processed foods are typically high in unhealthy fats, sugars, and additives, which can exacerbate inflammation and digestive issues. Avoid packaged snacks, cookies, cakes, and sugary cereals. Instead, opt for whole, unprocessed foods that are easier on the digestive system.
- **Red Meat and Fatty Proteins:** Fatty cuts of meat, such as beef, lamb, and pork, as well as processed meats like bacon, sausage, and hot dogs, are high

in saturated fats. These should be avoided in favor of lean proteins like chicken, turkey, and fish.
- **Alcohol:** Alcohol is a major trigger for both acute and chronic pancreatitis. It irritates the pancreas and can lead to severe inflammation, pain, and complications. Complete avoidance of alcohol is highly recommended for anyone with pancreatitis.
- **Spicy and Acidic Foods:** Highly spiced or acidic foods, such as spicy sauces, citrus fruits, and tomatoes, can irritate the pancreas and worsen symptoms. Stick to milder flavors and avoid foods that might provoke discomfort.

By embracing these healing foods and avoiding harmful ones, individuals with pancreatitis can manage their symptoms more effectively and promote long-term pancreatic health.

Stocking Your Pancreatitis Friendly Kitchen

Friendly Pantry Essentials

Building a friendly pantry is one of the most crucial steps for anyone living with pancreatitis. The right ingredients not only help manage the condition but also make cooking more convenient and enjoyable. Stocking your pantry with the proper staples ensures you have what you need to create meals that are both delicious and easy on the pancreas. Here are the essentials every pancreatitis-friendly kitchen should include:

- **Whole Grains:** Whole grains are a fundamental component of a healthy diet, especially for those with pancreatitis. They are rich in fiber, which aids digestion and stabilizes blood sugar levels. Keeping a variety of whole grains like brown rice, quinoa, oats, and barley in your pantry provides a versatile base for meals. These grains are easy to prepare and can be used in everything from breakfast porridge to dinner side dishes.
- **Low-Sodium Broth:** Having low-sodium broth on hand is incredibly useful for creating soups, stews, and other easy-to-digest meals. Broth adds flavor without relying on heavy fats or oils, and the low-sodium variety is better for your overall health. Look for broths that are low in fat and made from natural ingredients, avoiding artificial additives or high salt content.
- **Canned or Dried Legumes:** Legumes such as lentils, chickpeas, and black beans are great sources of plant-based protein and fiber. They're also low in fat, making them a fantastic addition to a pancreatitis-friendly diet. Stock both canned (low-sodium) and dried varieties to use in soups, salads, and main dishes. These legumes are not only nutritious but also filling, helping you feel satisfied without triggering symptoms.
- **Herbs and Spices:** Flavor is key to keeping meals interesting, especially when you're managing a restricted diet. Stocking your pantry with a variety of herbs and spices ensures that your meals remain flavorful without relying on fats, salt, or processed sauces. Essential spices for a pancreatitis-friendly diet include turmeric, ginger, cinnamon, and paprika. These spices also have anti-inflammatory properties, providing additional benefits beyond taste.
- **Healthy Oils (in Moderation):** While a low-fat diet is critical for managing pancreatitis, small amounts of healthy fats are necessary for overall health. Stock your pantry with olive oil or avocado oil, both of which are rich in omega-3 fatty acids and are easier to digest compared to saturated fats. Use these oils sparingly when cooking or dressings to maintain a balance between flavor and health.
- **Low-Fat Canned Tuna and Salmon:** Canned fish, such as tuna and salmon, are excellent sources of lean protein and healthy omega-3 fatty acids. Opt for varieties that are packed in water rather than oil to keep fat content low. These pantry staples are perfect for

creating quick meals like salads, sandwiches, or light pastas.

- **Canned Vegetables and Fruits:** Stocking canned vegetables and fruits ensures you always have something healthy on hand when fresh produce isn't available. Look for options that are low in sodium (for vegetables) and packed in water or juice (for fruits), avoiding any varieties that come with added sugars or preservatives. Canned tomatoes, peas, and green beans are great options for easy meals.

By ensuring that your pantry is stocked with these gut-friendly essentials, you'll always have the building blocks for nutritious meals that are gentle on your pancreas. When you have these staples on hand, it becomes easier to resist the temptation of reaching for unhealthy or high-fat foods.

Low-Fat Cooking Staples

Cooking for pancreatitis requires being mindful of fat intake, but that doesn't mean you have to sacrifice taste or variety. Stocking your kitchen with low-fat staples allows you to prepare meals that are not only delicious but also compliant with a pancreatitis-friendly diet. Here are some low-fat cooking staples that every kitchen should have:

- **Low-Fat Dairy Products:** Dairy is an important source of calcium, but high-fat varieties can be problematic for those with pancreatitis. Instead, opt for low-fat yogurt, skim milk, low-fat cottage cheese, and reduced-fat cheese. These dairy products provide essential nutrients without overloading your system with fat. They're also versatile—use yogurt in smoothies, cottage cheese in salads, or low-fat milk in baking.

- **Egg Whites:** Whole eggs are high in fat, which can trigger pancreatitis symptoms, but egg whites are a fantastic alternative. They're high in protein and completely fat-free. Keep cartons of egg whites in your fridge for easy breakfasts or add them to baked goods and casseroles for an extra protein boost without the added fat.

- **Lean Meats:** Protein is essential for maintaining muscle and supporting recovery, but not all sources of protein are suitable for pancreatitis. Stock your kitchen with skinless chicken breast, turkey, and lean cuts of pork. These meats are low in fat and easy to digest. Be sure to prepare them using low-fat cooking methods such as grilling, baking, or poaching to keep meals light and healthy.

- **Fat-Free Cooking Sprays:** When cooking, it's easy to accidentally add too much oil or butter, increasing the fat content of your meals. Fat-free cooking sprays are an excellent alternative that allow you to lightly coat your pans without adding unnecessary fat. These sprays are ideal for stir-fries, roasting, or sautéing vegetables and meats.

- **Fat-Free or Low-Fat Dressings and Sauces:** Sauces and dressings can often be a hidden source of fat, but fat-free and low-fat versions allow you to enjoy your favorite flavors without the added fat. Look for options like fat-free vinaigrettes, low-fat mayonnaise, and sugar-free ketchup to use in salads, marinades, or as condiments.

- **Low-Fat Whole Wheat Bread and Pasta:** Carbohydrates are an important source of energy, and whole wheat options provide more fiber and nutrients than refined grains. Stock your pantry with whole wheat bread, whole grain pasta, and brown rice. These are low in fat and high in fiber, making them perfect for meals that support digestion while keeping your pancreas at ease.
- **Unsweetened Applesauce:** Unsweetened applesauce is a great substitute for oil in baking recipes, adding moisture and flavor without the extra fat. It can also be eaten on its own as a healthy snack or mixed into oatmeal or yogurt for added sweetness.

With these low-fat cooking staples, you can easily create meals that are both satisfying and safe for managing pancreatitis. The key is to choose ingredients that provide nutrition while keeping fat content to a minimum.

Tools and Tips for Simplified Cooking

Having the right tools in your kitchen can make cooking for pancreatitis easier, faster, and more enjoyable. Simplified cooking doesn't mean compromising on taste or variety; it means using tools and techniques that reduce stress and time in the kitchen. Here are essential tools and tips to streamline your cooking process:

- **Non-Stick Cookware:** Non-stick pans and pots are a lifesaver for anyone trying to reduce their fat intake. With non-stick surfaces, you can cook with minimal oil or fat-free cooking spray, making it easier to prepare low-fat meals. Non-stick cookware also ensures that your food won't stick to the pan, reducing the likelihood of burning and making cleanup a breeze.
- **Steamer Basket:** Steaming is one of the healthiest cooking methods for pancreatitis-friendly meals because it retains nutrients and requires no added fats. A steamer basket allows you to cook vegetables, fish, and even poultry with ease. It's a gentle cooking method that helps preserve the delicate flavors and textures of food, making it perfect for a low-fat diet.
- **Blender or Food Processor:** A blender or food processor is invaluable for creating purees, smoothies, soups, and sauces. These tools make it easy to blend ingredients into a smooth consistency, which can be easier to digest for those with pancreatitis. You can also use them to prepare nut butters or hummus without the need for added oils.
- **Slow Cooker:** Slow cookers are perfect for making tender, flavorful meals with minimal effort. They allow you to cook dishes like soups, stews, and lean meats slowly over several hours, which not only intensifies flavors but also makes the food easier to digest. Simply throw in your ingredients in the morning, and by dinner time, you'll have a perfectly cooked, low-fat meal.
- **Meal Prep Containers:** Investing in meal prep containers makes it easy to portion out meals in advance, ensuring you always have a healthy option ready to go. Look for containers that are microwave- and

freezer-safe, allowing you to store meals for days when you don't have time to cook. Meal prepping can be a lifesaver for maintaining a pancreatitis-friendly diet while keeping your routine stress-free.
- **Sharp Knives:** A good set of sharp knives is essential for preparing healthy meals quickly and efficiently. Whether you're chopping vegetables, slicing lean meats, or dicing fruits, sharp knives reduce prep time and make it easier to handle your ingredients. Keep your knives sharp with a knife sharpener or honing steel to avoid frustration and improve safety in the kitchen.
- **Digital Scale:** If you're trying to monitor your portions closely to keep your fat intake low, a digital kitchen scale can be a helpful tool. It allows you to accurately measure ingredients like meats, oils, and grains, ensuring that you stay within recommended serving sizes for managing pancreatitis.

By using these tools and tips, you'll find that cooking for a pancreatitis-friendly diet is not only manageable but also enjoyable. Simplifying the cooking process ensures that you can focus on creating meals that are delicious, healthy, and easy on the pancreas.

Meal Prep Techniques to Save Time

Meal prepping is one of the best strategies for maintaining a healthy diet while managing pancreatitis. With some thoughtful planning and preparation, you can ensure that you always have nutritious, low-fat meals ready to go, even on your busiest days. Here are meal prep techniques that will save you time and help you stay on track with your diet:

- **Batch Cooking:** One of the easiest ways to save time during the week is by batch cooking your meals in advance. Choose a day when you have extra time, such as Sunday, and prepare large quantities of key ingredients like quinoa, brown rice, steamed vegetables, and lean meats. Store these in the fridge or freezer in meal-sized portions, so you have the building blocks for quick meals throughout the week.
- **Create a Weekly Meal Plan:** Planning your meals for the entire week ensures that you won't have to scramble for ideas or rely on unhealthy options when you're pressed for time. Write out your meal plan, including breakfast, lunch, dinner, and snacks. This will also help you create a focused grocery list so that you buy exactly what you need, reducing waste and saving time. To make things even easier, we've included a 7-day meal plan in this book, providing you with balanced and delicious options for each day, so you won't have to worry about creating your own meal plan from scratch.
- **Prep Ingredients in Advance:** Sometimes the hardest part of cooking is the prep work. Dedicate time to prepping your ingredients in advance. Wash and chop your vegetables, marinate your proteins, and measure out your grains ahead of time. Store them in containers in the fridge, so when it's time to cook, everything is ready to go.

- **Portion Your Meals:** After cooking, divide your meals into pre-portioned containers. This makes it easy to grab a meal when you're hungry without having to think about portion sizes. Having meals already portioned out ensures that you stick to the appropriate serving sizes and avoid overeating.
- **Utilize Freezer Meals:** Freezer-friendly meals like soups, stews, and casseroles can be made in large batches and stored in the freezer for future use. Simply pull a portion out of the freezer, thaw, and reheat for a quick and easy meal. Freezing meals is especially helpful on days when you're too busy or fatigued to cook.
- **Double Your Recipes:** Whenever you cook a meal, consider doubling the recipe. This way, you can enjoy one portion fresh and store the other in the fridge or freezer for later in the week. By doubling recipes, you save time on cooking and ensure that you always have something healthy on hand.

By incorporating these meal prep techniques into your routine, you can make eating for pancreatitis easier and more sustainable. Meal prepping not only saves time but also helps you avoid last-minute unhealthy food choices that could exacerbate your condition. With a little planning and preparation, you'll always have healthy, gut-friendly meals at your fingertips.

2

Nourishing Breakfasts to Kickstart Healing

Introduction to Nourishing Breakfast

Starting your day with a wholesome, nutrient-packed breakfast is essential, especially when managing pancreatitis. A well-balanced meal not only provides the energy you need to begin your day but also plays a crucial role in supporting pancreatic health. The following breakfast recipes are carefully crafted to be gentle on the pancreas, packed with essential nutrients, and full of flavor without compromising on satisfaction. Each recipe includes easy-to-find ingredients and detailed, step-by-step instructions to ensure your morning routine is as simple as possible. We've also placed a strong emphasis on keeping fat content low, making these dishes not only delicious but also safe and suitable for managing pancreatitis. Whether you prefer something sweet or savory, these options will provide you with the nourishment and comfort you need to kickstart your day on the right note, while prioritizing your health. Let's dive into these flavorful, pancreas-friendly breakfast options designed to keep your mornings stress-free and nutritious.

Creamy Oatmeal with Stewed Apples

- **Time of Preparation:** 10 minutes
- **Cooking Time:** 15 minutes
- **Serving Units:** 2 servings

Ingredients

- One cup of rolled oats, if needed gluten-free
- 2 cups water or unsweetened almond milk
- 1 apple, peeled, cored, and sliced
- 1 teaspoon cinnamon
- One teaspoon of optional maple syrup added for sweetness
- 1 tablespoon ground flaxseeds (optional, for added fiber)

Procedure

- Heat the almond milk or water in a medium saucepan until it begins to boil. Once boiling, add the oats and reduce the heat to low. Simmer for 10-12 minutes, stirring occasionally until the oats are creamy and cooked through.
- In a small skillet, add the sliced apple, cinnamon, and a splash of water. Cook over medium heat for 5-7 minutes until the apples are soft and tender. Stir in the maple syrup if you prefer a sweeter flavor.
- Serve the oatmeal in bowls, topped with the stewed apples and ground flaxseeds for an extra nutritional boost.

Nutritional Values (Per Serving)

- **Calories:** 220
- **Protein:** 5g
- **Fat:** 3g (from flaxseeds, if added)
- **Carbohydrates:** 45g
- **Fiber:** 8g
- **Sugar:** 8g

Cooking Tips

- If you prefer your oatmeal thicker, reduce the liquid slightly or simmer for a few extra minutes.
- For an added protein boost, consider stirring in a spoonful of low-fat Greek yogurt after cooking.

- Feel free to swap the apple for pears or peaches if you want variety.

Health Benefits

- Oats are rich in soluble fiber, which helps stabilize blood sugar levels and supports digestive health.
- Apples provide a good source of fiber and antioxidants, making them ideal for calming inflammation.
- Flaxseeds are a great source of omega-3 fatty acids and fiber, promoting heart and gut health.

Fluffy Egg White Scramble with Spinach

- **Time of Preparation:** 5 minutes
- **Cooking Time:** 5 minutes
- **Serving Units:** 1 serving

Ingredients

- 4 egg whites
- 1 cup fresh spinach, chopped
- 1 tablespoon unsweetened almond milk (optional, for fluffiness)
- One teaspoon of non-stick spray or olive oil
- Salt and pepper to taste
- 1 tablespoon fresh herbs (such as parsley or chives, optional)

Procedure

- In a medium bowl, whisk the egg whites and almond milk until frothy.
- Heat a non-stick skillet over medium heat and lightly coat it with olive oil or spray.
- When the spinach has wilted, add it and sauté it for one to two minutes.
- Pour in the egg whites and cook, stirring gently, for about 3-4 minutes until the eggs are fully cooked and fluffy. If desired, add herbs, salt, and pepper for seasoning.
- Serve warm, alongside whole wheat toast or a side of fresh fruit.

Nutritional Values (Per Serving)

- **Calories:** 90
- **Protein:** 16g
- **Fat:** 2g
- **Carbohydrates:** 2g
- **Fiber:** 1g
- **Sugar:** 1g

Cooking Tips

- Using unsweetened almond milk in the egg whites adds fluffiness, making the scramble lighter.
- Add any other gentle-on-the-pancreas veggies like diced bell peppers or mushrooms for extra nutrition.
- Be sure not to overcook the eggs—scrambled egg whites should be light and tender, not rubbery.

Health Benefits

- Egg whites are a lean source of protein, which is crucial for tissue repair and maintaining muscle mass without the fat found in whole eggs.
- Spinach is loaded with vitamins A and C, iron, and fiber, all of which support a healthy immune system and digestion.
- This meal is low in fat, making it gentle on the pancreas while providing high-quality protein to fuel your day.

Banana Chia Pudding

- **Time of Preparation:** 5 minutes (plus overnight refrigeration)
- **Cooking Time:** None
- **Serving Units:** 2 servings

Ingredients

- 1 large banana, mashed
- 2 tablespoons chia seeds
- 1 cup unsweetened almond milk
- 1 teaspoon vanilla extract
- 1 teaspoon maple syrup (optional)
- Fresh fruit or berries for topping (optional)

Procedure

- Mash the banana in a small bowl until it's smooth. Stir in the chia seeds, almond milk, vanilla extract, and maple syrup if desired.
- Transfer the mixture to a mason jar or airtight container, cover, and refrigerate overnight (or at least 4 hours) to allow the chia seeds to absorb the liquid and form a pudding-like texture.
- In the morning, give the pudding a good stir. Serve topped with fresh fruit or berries for added flavor and nutrients.

Nutritional Values (Per Serving)

- **Calories:** 180
- **Protein:** 4g
- **Fat:** 6g
- **Carbohydrates:** 30g
- **Fiber:** 8g
- **Sugar:** 10g

Cooking Tips

- If you prefer a smoother texture, blend the chia pudding mixture before refrigerating it for a more consistent consistency.
- Chia seeds can absorb a lot of liquid, so adjust the amount of almond milk if you prefer a thinner or thicker pudding.
- Add a sprinkle of cinnamon or a dash of cocoa powder for extra flavor without adding fat.

Health Benefits

- Chia seeds are a great source of fiber and healthy omega-3 fatty acids, which support digestive health and help reduce inflammation.
- Bananas provide potassium, which helps balance fluid levels in the body and supports nerve and muscle function.
- This easy-to-digest, low-fat pudding is packed with nutrients that support gut health and provide steady energy throughout the morning.

Soothing Smoothie Bowls

- **Time of Preparation:** 10 minutes
- **Cooking Time:** None
- **Serving Units:** 2 servings

Ingredients

- 1 frozen banana
- 1/2 cup of unsweetened coconut water or almond milk
- 1/2 cup plain low-fat yogurt (optional for added creaminess)
- 1/4 cup oats
- Half a cup of frozen fruit, such strawberries or blueberries
- 1 tablespoon chia seeds
- Toppings: sliced kiwi, fresh berries, shredded coconut, or granola (optional)

Procedure

- In a high-speed blender, combine the frozen banana, almond milk, yogurt (if using), oats, frozen berries, and chia seeds. Blend until smooth and creamy.
- Pour the smoothie mixture into bowls.
- Top with your choice of toppings such as fresh berries, sliced kiwi, shredded coconut, or a small sprinkle of granola for crunch. Serve immediately.

Nutritional Values (Per Serving)

- **Calories:** 250
- **Protein:** 8g
- **Fat:** 6g
- **Carbohydrates:** 45g
- **Fiber:** 10g
- **Sugar:** 18g

Cooking Tips

- The key to a thick, creamy smoothie bowl is using frozen fruit. If your smoothie is too thin, add more frozen banana or berries to thicken it.
- For an extra protein boost, you can add a scoop of low-fat Greek yogurt or a protein powder specifically designed for those with digestive sensitivities.
- Be mindful with toppings—stick to fresh fruit, shredded coconut, or a small amount of granola to keep the fat content low.

Health Benefits

- Frozen berries are full of antioxidants that reduce inflammation and protect cells from damage.
- Bananas provide fiber and essential nutrients like potassium, supporting gut and heart health.
- This smoothie bowl is rich in fiber, which aids digestion, and offers a nutrient-dense, low-fat start to your day that's gentle on the pancreas.

Each of these breakfast recipes is designed to nourish your body and support healing without compromising on flavor. They are quick to prepare, making them perfect for busy mornings, while also being low in fat, making them gentle on the digestive system. From creamy oatmeal to refreshing smoothie bowls, these recipes provide the energy and nutrients you need to kickstart your day in a way that supports long-term health. Whether you're looking for a warm breakfast or something cold and refreshing, these options will make breakfast both enjoyable and nutritious.

3

Light and Satisfying Lunches

Frank J. Weston

Lunch is an important meal that can provide the fuel you need to power through the rest of your day. For individuals managing pancreatitis, light but satisfying options are ideal, with a focus on nutrient-dense foods that are gentle on the digestive system. It's essential to prioritize meals that are low in fat, rich in lean proteins, and packed with vitamins and minerals to promote healing and maintain energy levels. Whether you're at home or on the go, preparing a balanced lunch doesn't have to be complicated. These recipes are not only easy to make but also flavorful and nourishing, ensuring that you can enjoy your meal while supporting your health. Below are delicious lunch recipes that are easy to prepare, packed with flavor, and filled with the essential nutrients your body needs to stay energized and healthy throughout the day.

Quinoa Salad with Cucumber and Avocado

- **Time of Preparation:** 10 minutes
- **Cooking Time:** 15 minutes
- **Serving Units:** 2 servings

Ingredients

- 1 cup quinoa, rinsed
- Two cups of water or vegetable broth low in sodium
- 1 medium cucumber, diced
- 1 ripe avocado, diced
- 1/4 cup finely chopped cilantro or parsley, fresh
- 1 tablespoon olive oil
- 1 tablespoon lemon juice
- Salt and pepper to taste

Procedure

- Bring the vegetable broth or water to a boil in a medium saucepan. When the quinoa is soft and the liquid has been absorbed, add it, lower the heat to low, cover, and simmer for 15 minutes. Turn off the heat and let it to cool.
- In a large bowl, combine the cooled quinoa, diced cucumber, avocado, and fresh parsley or cilantro.
- Mix the lemon juice, olive oil, salt, and pepper in a small bowl. After adding the dressing to the salad, gently toss to mix.
- Serve chilled or at room temperature for a light and refreshing lunch.

Nutritional Values (Per Serving)

- **Calories:** 320
- **Protein:** 8g
- **Fat:** 18g
- **Carbohydrates:** 36g
- **Fiber:** 9g
- **Sugar:** 2g

Cooking Tips

- To eliminate the quinoa's inherent bitterness, make sure you give it a good rinse before cooking.
-
- You can prepare the quinoa in advance and store it in the fridge, making it easy to assemble this salad on busy days.

- For added crunch, consider adding a handful of sunflower seeds or pumpkin seeds (if tolerated).

Health Benefits

- Quinoa is a complete protein, containing all nine essential amino acids, making it an excellent plant-based protein source for those managing pancreatitis.
- Avocado provides healthy fats and fiber, both of which support heart and digestive health. Its creamy texture also makes the salad more satisfying.
- The cucumber adds hydration and lightness, helping to balance the meal and keep it refreshing.

Chicken and Sweet Potato Lettuce Wraps

- **Time of Preparation:** 10 minutes
- **Cooking Time:** 30 minutes
- **Serving Units:** 4 wraps

Ingredients

- One medium-sized sweet potato, diced and peeling
- 2 boneless, skinless chicken breasts
- 1 tablespoon olive oil
- 1 teaspoon paprika
- Salt and pepper to taste
- 8 large lettuce leaves (such as Romaine or butter lettuce)
- 1/4 cup plain low-fat yogurt (optional, for serving)
- Fresh cilantro for garnish (optional)

Procedure

- Preheat your oven to 400°F (200°C). Toss the cubed sweet potatoes with 1/2 tablespoon olive oil, paprika, salt, and pepper. Spread them on a baking sheet and roast for 25-30 minutes until tender and golden.
- Meanwhile, heat the remaining olive oil in a skillet over medium heat. Season the chicken breasts with salt and pepper, and cook for 6-7 minutes per side until fully cooked through. Let the chicken rest for 5 minutes, then slice it thinly.
- To assemble the wraps, lay a few slices of chicken and roasted sweet potatoes on each lettuce leaf. Top with a spoonful of low-fat yogurt and sprinkle with fresh cilantro, if desired.
- Roll up the lettuce wraps and enjoy!

Nutritional Values (Per Serving)

- **Calories:** 280
- **Protein:** 28g
- **Fat:** 10g
- **Carbohydrates:** 21g
- **Fiber:** 5g
- **Sugar:** 5g

Cooking Tips

- Swap the chicken for grilled tofu or turkey breast if you prefer a different protein.
- Roasting the sweet potatoes brings out their natural sweetness and makes

them soft enough to pair well with the crunchy lettuce.
- These wraps are great for meal prepping—just store the components separately and assemble when ready to eat.

Health Benefits

- Sweet potatoes are rich in vitamins A and C, which are vital for immune function and skin health, and they provide a gentle source of carbohydrates for energy.
- Chicken breast offers lean protein, helping repair tissues and maintain muscle mass without overloading your system with fat.
- Lettuce wraps are a low-carb, low-calorie alternative to bread or tortillas, keeping this meal light while still satisfying.

Lentil and Vegetable Soup

- **Time of Preparation:** 10 minutes
- **Cooking Time:** 35 minutes
- **Serving Units:** 4 servings

Ingredients

- 1 cup dried green or brown lentils, rinsed
- 1 onion, finely chopped
- 2 carrots, peeled and chopped
- 2 celery stalks, chopped
- 2 garlic cloves, minced
- 1 teaspoon cumin
- 6 cups low-sodium vegetable broth
- 1 bay leaf
- 2 cups chopped spinach or kale
- Salt and pepper to taste
- Lemon wedges for serving

Procedure

- In a large pot, sauté the onion, carrots, celery, and garlic over medium heat for 5-7 minutes until softened.
- Stir in the cumin and cook for another minute to release its flavor.
- Add the lentils, vegetable broth, and bay leaf. After bringing to a boil, lower the heat and simmer the lentils for 30 to 35 minutes, or until they become soft.
- Stir in the chopped spinach or kale and cook for another 5 minutes until wilted. Season with salt and pepper to taste.
- Remove the bay leaf and serve the soup with a wedge of lemon on the side for a bright, fresh finish.

Nutritional Values (Per Serving)

- **Calories:** 210
- **Protein:** 12g
- **Fat:** 2g
- **Carbohydrates:** 36g
- **Fiber:** 14g
- **Sugar:** 4g

Cooking Tips

- Lentils don't need to be soaked beforehand, making them a quick and convenient ingredient for soups.
- Feel free to switch up the veggies based on what's in season—zucchini, bell

peppers, or tomatoes would also work well.
- For a creamier texture, blend half the soup and stir it back in.

Health Benefits

- Lentils are high in plant-based protein and fiber, which support digestive health and help maintain steady energy levels.
- Spinach and kale add a boost of vitamins K and A, as well as antioxidants that help reduce inflammation.
- This soup is low in fat and easy to digest, making it a great option for individuals managing pancreatitis.

Grilled Zucchini and Hummus Wrap

- **Time of Preparation:** 10 minutes
- **Cooking Time:** 10 minutes
- **Serving Units:** 2 servings

Ingredients

- 2 medium zucchinis, sliced lengthwise
- 2 tablespoons olive oil
- Salt and pepper to taste
- 4 whole wheat tortillas
- 1/2 cup hummus (store-bought or homemade)
- 1/4 cup shredded carrots
- 1/4 cup thinly sliced bell peppers
- 1 tablespoon fresh lemon juice
- Fresh parsley or cilantro for garnish

Procedure

- Set an outside grill or grill pan on medium heat. Add salt and pepper to the zucchini slices after brushing them with olive oil. Grill for 3-4 minutes per side until tender and lightly charred.
- Each tortilla should have two teaspoons of hummus on it. Top with grilled zucchini, shredded carrots, and bell peppers.
- Drizzle with lemon juice and sprinkle fresh parsley or cilantro on top for extra freshness.
- Serve the wraps right away after rolling them up.

Nutritional Values (Per Serving)

- **Calories:** 350
- **Protein:** 10g
- **Fat:** 15g
- **Carbohydrates:** 44g
- **Fiber:** 8g
- **Sugar:** 5g

Cooking Tips

- If you don't have a grill, you can roast the zucchini in the oven at 400°F (200°C) for about 10 minutes.
- Feel free to add other grilled veggies, such as eggplant or mushrooms, to make the wrap heartier.
- For a gluten-free option, use lettuce leaves or gluten-free wraps instead of whole wheat tortillas.

Health Benefits

- Zucchini is low in calories and packed with water, making it easy to digest while still providing fiber, vitamins, and minerals.
- Hummus is rich in protein and healthy fats from chickpeas and tahini, helping to keep you satisfied without triggering inflammation.
- The whole wheat tortillas provide fiber and complex carbohydrates, giving you steady energy throughout the day.

These light and satisfying lunches are ideal for anyone looking to support their pancreatic health while enjoying flavorful, nutrient-packed meals. Each dish is quick to prepare, making them perfect for busy days, and they offer a balance of healthy proteins, fibers, and low-fat ingredients. Whether you're craving a refreshing quinoa salad or a comforting bowl of lentil soup, these recipes will leave you feeling nourished, energized, and ready to take on the rest of your day.

4

Wholesome Snacks for Pancreatic Relief

Frank J. Weston

Snacks can be an essential part of managing your energy levels and keeping your digestive system running smoothly throughout the day. For individuals with pancreatitis, it's crucial to choose snacks that are not only gentle on the pancreas but also nourishing and satisfying. It's important to avoid snacks that are high in fats, processed sugars, or additives, as these can place unnecessary stress on your digestive system. Instead, focus on simple, whole foods that are rich in vitamins, minerals, and lean protein, which will help support your body without aggravating your condition. Below are snacks ideas that are quick to prepare, packed with nutrients, and designed to provide relief and support for your pancreas, ensuring you stay energized and well-nourished throughout the day while keeping your symptoms in check.

Baked Apple Slices with Cinnamon

- **Time of Preparation:** 5 minutes
- **Cooking Time:** 20 minutes
- **Serving Units:** 2 servings

Ingredients

- 2 medium apples, peeled, cored, and sliced
- 1 teaspoon ground cinnamon
- 1 teaspoon honey (optional)
- A pinch of nutmeg (optional)

Procedure

- Preheat the oven to 375°F (190°C). Line a baking sheet with parchment paper.
- Place the apple slices in a single layer on the baking sheet that has been preheated.
- Sprinkle the cinnamon (and nutmeg, if using) evenly over the apple slices.
- Bake for 18-20 minutes until the apples are soft and slightly golden around the edges.
- If you like a touch of sweetness, drizzle a little honey over the apples before serving. Enjoy warm or at room temperature.

Nutritional Values (Per Serving)

- **Calories:** 90
- **Protein:** 0g
- **Fat:** 0g
- **Carbohydrates:** 25g
- **Fiber:** 4g
- **Sugar:** 19g (natural sugar from apples)

Cooking Tips

- For added flavor, consider adding a dash of vanilla extract before baking.
- If you want the apple slices crisper, bake them for an extra 5 minutes, keeping a close eye to avoid burning.
- This snack can also be served with a dollop of low-fat Greek yogurt for added creaminess and protein.

Health Benefits

- Apples are an excellent source of dietary fiber, which aids digestion and promotes gut health. The natural

- pectin in apples helps soothe the digestive tract.
- Cinnamon is known for its anti-inflammatory properties, which may help reduce inflammation associated with pancreatitis.
- This snack is low in fat and easy on the pancreas, making it ideal for mid-morning or afternoon breaks.

Rice Cakes with Avocado Spread

- **Time of Preparation:** 5 minutes
- **Cooking Time:** None
- **Serving Units:** 2 servings

Ingredients

- 4 plain rice cakes (whole grain or brown rice preferred)
- 1 ripe avocado, mashed
- 1 tablespoon lemon juice
- Salt and pepper to taste
- A pinch of red pepper flakes (optional, for mild heat)

Procedure

- Mash the avocado with the lemon juice, salt, and pepper in a small bowl. Add red pepper flakes if you enjoy a slight kick of heat.
- Spread the avocado mixture evenly over the rice cakes.
- Serve immediately, topped with fresh herbs or a sprinkle of seeds (optional).

Nutritional Values (Per Serving)

- **Calories:** 160
- **Protein:** 3g
- **Fat:** 9g
- **Carbohydrates:** 20g
- **Fiber:** 5g
- **Sugar:** 0g

Cooking Tips:

- Be sure to use ripe avocado for the smoothest spread. If the avocado is too firm, add a splash of olive oil or yogurt for added creaminess.
- You can switch up the toppings to add more flavor or nutrition. Consider adding sliced tomatoes, radishes, or cucumbers for extra crunch.
- Rice cakes can go stale quickly once opened, so store them in an airtight container to maintain freshness.

Health Benefits

- Avocados are rich in healthy monounsaturated fats, which are easier for the body to digest compared to saturated fats, making them suitable for a pancreatitis-friendly diet.

- Rice cakes provide a low-fat, gluten-free base that adds texture without overwhelming your system.
- The combination of fiber and healthy fats keeps you satisfied between meals while supporting heart and digestive health.

Greek Yogurt with Blueberries and Honey

- **Time of Preparation:** 5 minutes
- **Cooking Time:** None
- **Serving Units:** 1 serving

Ingredients

- 1/2 cup plain low-fat Greek yogurt
- 1/4 cup fresh blueberries
- 1 teaspoon honey
- 1 tablespoon ground flaxseeds (optional, for added fiber)

Procedure

- Greek yogurt should be spooned into a bowl.
- Top with fresh blueberries and drizzle the honey over the top.
- If desired, sprinkle ground flaxseeds for an extra boost of fiber and omega-3s.
- Serve immediately and enjoy!

Nutritional Values (Per Serving):

- **Calories:** 150
- **Protein:** 10g
- **Fat:** 2g
- **Carbohydrates:** 24g
- **Fiber:** 4g
- **Sugar:** 15g

Cooking Tips:

- If you prefer a bit more sweetness, feel free to increase the honey to 2 teaspoons. Just be aware of the sugar addition.
- You can substitute the blueberries with other berries like strawberries or raspberries, depending on what's in season.
- Make this snack more filling by adding a handful of granola or chia seeds.

Health Benefits

- Greek yogurt is an excellent source of protein and probiotics, which promote gut health and aid digestion. Low-fat options are ideal for reducing the burden on the pancreas.

- Blueberries are packed with antioxidants, particularly vitamin C, which help reduce inflammation in the body.
- A drizzle of honey provides natural sweetness and a quick source of energy without overwhelming the digestive system.

Cucumber and Carrot Sticks with Yogurt Dip

- **Time of Preparation:** 10 minutes
- **Cooking Time:** None
- **Serving Units:** 2 servings

Ingredients

- 1 medium cucumber, cut into sticks
- 2 medium carrots, peeled and cut into sticks
- 1/2 cup plain low-fat Greek yogurt
- 1 teaspoon lemon juice
- 1/2 teaspoon garlic powder
- 1 teaspoon fresh dill, chopped (optional)
- Salt and pepper to taste

Procedure

- In a small bowl, mix the Greek yogurt, lemon juice, garlic powder, dill, salt, and pepper until well combined.
- Arrange the cucumber and carrot sticks on a plate and serve with the yogurt dip on the side.
- Enjoy the crunchy veggies dipped in the creamy yogurt mixture for a refreshing snack.

Nutritional Values (Per Serving)

- **Calories:** 90
- **Protein:** 5g
- **Fat:** 2g
- **Carbohydrates:** 15g
- **Fiber:** 4g
- **Sugar:** 7g

Cooking Tips:

- If you want to add variety, include other vegetables like celery sticks, bell pepper slices, or cherry tomatoes.
- The yogurt dip can be made ahead and stored in the refrigerator for up to 3 days. Before serving, just give it a quick swirl.
- For a creamier dip, you can use low-fat sour cream mixed with yogurt.

Health Benefits

- Cucumbers and carrots are both rich in fiber and water content, which help with digestion and hydration. Their

natural crunch also makes them a satisfying low-calorie snack.
- The yogurt dip adds a boost of protein and probiotics, supporting gut health and making the snack more filling.
- This snack is light but loaded with nutrients, making it ideal for curbing hunger without taxing your digestive system.

These wholesome snacks are not only easy to prepare but are also gentle on the pancreas, making them perfect options for people managing pancreatitis. Each snack is packed with nutrients that support your digestive system, reduce inflammation, and keep your energy levels steady throughout the day. Whether you're in the mood for something sweet like baked apple slices or savory like cucumber sticks with yogurt dip, these snacks will leave you feeling satisfied and well-nourished.

5

Low-Fat Main Courses

Low-fat main courses are not only essential for those managing conditions like pancreatitis, but they also play a vital role in supporting overall health and wellness. By emphasizing lean proteins, whole grains, and fiber-packed vegetables, these dishes are designed to be light yet filling, providing the necessary nutrients without burdening the digestive system. Whether you're aiming to reduce fat intake for medical reasons or simply striving for a more balanced diet, these recipes deliver delicious, wholesome meals that are both satisfying and easy to make. Each recipe has been carefully crafted to ensure it meets dietary needs while still delivering on flavor, texture, and variety, making it easier to enjoy nourishing meals every day. Below, you'll discover four diverse main courses that perfectly balance health and taste, proving that eating low-fat doesn't mean sacrificing the joy of eating.

Poached Chicken Breast with Steamed Veggies

- **Time of Preparation:** 10 minutes
- **Cooking Time:** 20 minutes
- **Serving Units:** 2 servings

Ingredients

- 2 boneless, skinless chicken breasts
- 1 bay leaf
- 1 garlic clove, crushed
- 1 teaspoon black peppercorns
- 2 cups low-sodium chicken broth (or water)
- 1 cup broccoli florets
- 1 cup carrot sticks
- 1 tablespoon olive oil
- Salt and pepper to taste
- Fresh parsley for garnish (optional)

Procedure

- In a medium saucepan, bring the chicken broth (or water), bay leaf, garlic, and peppercorns to a simmer. After adding, make sure the chicken breasts are completely submerged. Reduce heat to low and poach for 12-15 minutes until the chicken is fully cooked and tender.
- While the chicken is poaching, set up a steamer basket over a pot of boiling water. Steam the broccoli and carrots for 5-7 minutes, until they are tender but still crisp.
- Remove the chicken from the broth, slice, and season with salt, pepper, and a drizzle of olive oil.
- Serve the poached chicken alongside the steamed vegetables, garnished with fresh parsley if desired.

Nutritional Values (Per Serving)

- **Calories:** 270
- **Protein:** 35g
- **Fat:** 10g
- **Carbohydrates:** 10g
- **Fiber:** 5g
- **Sugar:** 5g

Cooking Tips

- To avoid drying out the chicken, make sure the poaching liquid stays at a gentle simmer and never boils.

- You can poach extra chicken breasts to use in salads, wraps, or sandwiches throughout the week.
- Feel free to swap in other vegetables like zucchini or cauliflower depending on what's in season.

Health Benefits

- Poaching the chicken in broth keeps it tender without adding unnecessary fats, making this method ideal for pancreatitis-friendly meals.
- Broccoli and carrots are rich in fiber, vitamins, and antioxidants that help reduce inflammation and support digestion.
- This dish provides a perfect balance of lean protein, healthy fats, and nutrient-dense vegetables, helping you feel satisfied without overloading your digestive system.

Grilled Salmon with Quinoa and Asparagus

- **Time of Preparation:** 10 minutes
- **Cooking Time:** 20 minutes
- **Serving Units:** 2 servings

Ingredients

- 2 salmon fillets (about 4 oz each)
- 1 cup quinoa, rinsed
- Two cups of water or vegetable broth low in sodium
- 1 bunch asparagus, trimmed
- 1 tablespoon olive oil
- 1 tablespoon lemon juice
- Salt and pepper to taste
- Fresh dill for garnish (optional)

Procedure

- Turn the heat up to medium-high on the grill or grill pan. Toss the salmon fillets with a little olive oil, salt, and pepper.
- Grill the salmon for 4-5 minutes per side until it flakes easily with a fork.
- While the salmon is grilling, bring the water or vegetable broth to a boil. Add the quinoa, reduce the heat to low, cover, and simmer for 15 minutes or until the quinoa is cooked and fluffy.
- Combine the asparagus with salt, pepper, and olive oil. Grill the asparagus for 4-5 minutes until tender and slightly charred.
- Serve the grilled salmon with quinoa and asparagus, drizzled with lemon juice and garnished with fresh dill.

Nutritional Values (Per Serving)

- **Calories:** 430
- **Protein:** 32g
- **Fat:** 18g
- **Carbohydrates:** 38g
- **Fiber:** 7g
- **Sugar:** 3g

Cooking Tips

- For added flavor, marinate the salmon for 15 minutes in a mixture of olive oil, lemon juice, and fresh herbs before grilling.

- If you don't have access to a grill, bake the salmon and asparagus in the oven at 400°F (200°C) for about 12-15 minutes.
- You can prepare extra quinoa and store it in the fridge for other meals throughout the week.

Health Benefits

- Salmon is an excellent source of omega-3 fatty acids, which help reduce inflammation and support heart health.
- Quinoa is a complete protein and a gluten-free grain that's rich in fiber, making it great for digestion and energy maintenance.
- Asparagus contains vitamins A, C, and K, as well as folate, supporting healthy digestion and overall well-being.

Baked Cod with Lemon and Herbs

- **Time of Preparation:** 5 minutes
- **Cooking Time:** 15 minutes
- **Serving Units:** 2 servings

Ingredients

- Two fillets of fish, about 4 oz each
- 1 tablespoon olive oil
- 2 tablespoons lemon juice
- 1 teaspoon dried thyme or oregano
- Salt and pepper to taste
- Lemon wedges for serving

Procedure

- Preheat the oven to 375°F (190°C). Line a baking sheet with parchment paper.
- Cod fillets should be placed on the ready baking sheet. Drizzle with olive oil and lemon juice, then season with thyme, salt, and pepper.
- Bake the cod for 12-15 minutes, or until it flakes easily with a fork.
- Serve the cod with lemon wedges and your choice of steamed vegetables or a side salad.

Nutritional Values (Per Serving)

- **Calories:** 200
- **Protein:** 25g
- **Fat:** 8g
- **Carbohydrates:** 4g
- **Fiber:** 0g
- **Sugar:** 0g

Cooking Tips

- If you prefer a crispy texture, you can broil the cod for the last 2-3 minutes of cooking time.
- For variety, try using different herbs like dill, parsley, or rosemary for seasoning.
- Cod is a mild-flavored fish that pairs well with various sides—try serving it with roasted potatoes or couscous.

Health Benefits

- Cod is a lean fish that's high in protein and low in fat, making it an ideal

choice for those managing pancreatitis.
- The lemon juice not only adds flavor but also provides vitamin C, which boosts the immune system and supports skin health.
- This meal is simple yet satisfying, offering a nutritious source of lean protein and healthy fats with minimal calories.

Turkey and Brown Rice Stuffed Bell Peppers

- **Time of Preparation:** 15 minutes
- **Cooking Time:** 35 minutes
- **Serving Units:** 4 servings

Ingredients

- 4 big bell peppers with the seeds removed and the tops removed
- 1/2 lb lean ground turkey
- 1 cup cooked brown rice
- 1 small onion, finely chopped
- 1 garlic clove, minced
- 1 teaspoon paprika
- 1/2 cup low-sodium tomato sauce
- 1 tablespoon olive oil
- Salt and pepper to taste
- Fresh parsley for garnish (optional)

Procedure

- Preheat the oven to 375°F (190°C). Place the bell peppers in a baking dish upright.
- Heat the olive oil in a big skillet over medium heat. Add the garlic and onion and sauté until they become tender. Once added, sauté the ground turkey until browned.
- Stir in the cooked brown rice, paprika, tomato sauce, salt, and pepper. Cook for 3-4 minutes to combine flavors.
- Stuff the turkey and rice mixture into each bell pepper. Bake the casserole, covered with foil, for 30 to 35 minutes, or until the peppers are soft.
- Garnish with fresh parsley before serving.

Nutritional Values (Per Serving)

- **Calories:** 290
- **Protein:** 25g
- **Fat:** 10g
- **Carbohydrates:** 30g
- **Fiber:** 5g
- **Sugar:** 6g

Cooking Tips

- If you have extra filling, use it to make wraps or as a topping for salads.

- You can substitute quinoa for brown rice if you prefer a higher-protein alternative.
- To save time, prepare the turkey and rice mixture in advance and stuff the peppers just before baking.

Health Benefits

- Lean ground turkey provides a high-protein, low-fat option that's easy to digest and supports muscle repair and maintenance.
- Brown rice is a whole grain that's rich in fiber, promoting digestive health and keeping you full for longer.
- Bell peppers are packed with vitamins A and C, providing antioxidants that help reduce inflammation and support immune function.

Each of these low-fat main courses is designed to offer flavor, variety, and vital nutrients while being easy on your digestive system. These recipes combine lean proteins, whole grains, and nutrient-dense vegetables to create balanced meals that not only support pancreatic health but also leave you feeling satisfied. Whether you're grilling salmon or baking stuffed bell peppers, you'll enjoy meals that are as nourishing as they are delicious.

6
Easy, Soothing Soups

Soups are a comforting and easy way to provide essential nutrients while being gentle on the digestive system, making them ideal for individuals managing pancreatitis. These soups are not only soothing but also packed with anti-inflammatory ingredients and fiber to promote healing and overall well-being. Carefully curated to avoid any ingredients that could trigger discomfort, each recipe focuses on balancing flavors with gentle, wholesome components that support digestive health. With a variety of vegetables, lean proteins, and healing spices, these soups deliver a satisfying meal without compromising on flavor or nutrition. Whether you're looking for something light or hearty, these nourishing options are easy to prepare, simple to digest, and full of vibrant flavors to help you feel your best. Below, you'll find four flavorful and nourishing soups that are simple to prepare, easy to digest, and full of vibrant flavors.

Carrot and Ginger Puree Soup

- **Time of Preparation:** 10 minutes
- **Cooking Time:** 20 minutes
- **Serving Units:** 4 servings

Ingredients

- 6 large carrots, peeled and chopped
- 1 small onion, chopped
- 1 tablespoon fresh ginger, grated
- 2 cups low-sodium vegetable broth
- 1 tablespoon olive oil
- Salt and pepper to taste
- Fresh parsley for garnish (optional)

Procedure

- Warm up the olive oil in a big saucepan over medium heat. Add the onions and sauté for 5-6 minutes until softened.
- Stir in the ginger and carrots, and sauté for another 2-3 minutes.
- Add the vegetable broth and bring the mixture to a boil. Once the carrots are soft, reduce the heat and simmer for 15 to 20 minutes.
- Blend the soup until it's smooth and creamy using an immersion blender or a conventional blender (in batches).
- To taste, add salt and pepper for seasoning. If preferred, garnish with fresh parsley and serve warm.

Nutritional Values (Per Serving)

- **Calories:** 110
- **Protein:** 2g
- **Fat:** 4g
- **Carbohydrates:** 17g
- **Fiber:** 5g
- **Sugar:** 9g

Cooking Tips

- If you prefer a slightly richer flavor, add a splash of coconut milk before blending.
- Grate the ginger finely to ensure a smooth texture and distribute its flavor evenly throughout the soup.
- For extra brightness, squeeze a little fresh lemon juice over the soup before serving.

Health Benefits

- Carrots are high in beta-carotene and vitamin A, which support immune function and eye health while promoting skin repair.
- Ginger is known for its anti-inflammatory and digestive properties, making it soothing for the stomach and helpful in reducing nausea or discomfort.
- This soup is low in calories and fat, making it ideal for a light meal that nourishes without overwhelming the digestive system.

Chicken and Rice Broth

- **Time of Preparation:** 10 minutes
- **Cooking Time:** 30 minutes
- **Serving Units:** 4 servings

Ingredients

- 2 boneless, skinless chicken breasts
- 1/2 cup white or brown rice, rinsed
- 1 small onion, chopped
- 2 celery stalks, chopped
- 1 carrot, chopped
- 6 cups low-sodium chicken broth
- 1 bay leaf
- Salt and pepper to taste
- Fresh parsley for garnish (optional)

Procedure

- In a large pot, bring the chicken broth, bay leaf, onion, celery, and carrot to a simmer.
- Add the chicken breasts and cook for 12-15 minutes, until fully cooked. Take out and place the chicken somewhere to cool.
- Add the rice to the broth and simmer for an additional 15 minutes until the rice is tender.
- Shred the cooked chicken and return it to the pot. Season with salt and pepper to taste.
- Remove the bay leaf before serving. Garnish with fresh parsley, if desired, and enjoy warm.

Nutritional Values (Per Serving)

- **Calories:** 250
- **Protein:** 25g
- **Fat:** 5g
- **Carbohydrates:** 25g
- **Fiber:** 3g
- **Sugar:** 3g

Cooking Tips

- If you prefer a thicker broth, use less liquid or add more rice.
- For a richer flavor, simmer the broth with a sprig of thyme or rosemary.
- You can make a larger batch and freeze individual portions for easy reheating on busy days.

Health Benefits

- Chicken breast is a lean source of protein, essential for tissue repair and muscle maintenance, while being gentle on the pancreas.
- Rice adds easily digestible carbohydrates to this soup, providing steady energy without overwhelming the digestive system.
- This broth is perfect for hydration and replenishing nutrients after a long day, while also being low in fat and easy on the stomach.

Creamy Cauliflower Soup

- **Time of Preparation:** 10 minutes
- **Cooking Time:** 25 minutes
- **Serving Units:** 4 servings

Ingredients

- 1 large head of cauliflower, chopped into florets
- 1 small onion, chopped
- 2 garlic cloves, minced
- 2 cups low-sodium vegetable broth
- 1 cup unsweetened almond milk
- 1 tablespoon olive oil
- Salt and pepper to taste
- Fresh thyme for garnish (optional)

Procedure

- In a big saucepan, warm up the olive oil over medium heat. Add the onion and garlic, sautéing for 5-6 minutes until fragrant and softened.
- Add the cauliflower florets and vegetable broth. After bringing to a boil, decrease the heat, and simmer the cauliflower for 20 minutes, or until it becomes soft.
- Stir in the almond milk and remove the soup from heat. Using an immersion blender, puree the soup until it's creamy and smooth.
- Season with salt and pepper to taste, and garnish with fresh thyme, if desired.

Nutritional Values (Per Serving)

- **Calories:** 140
- **Protein:** 4g
- **Fat:** 6g
- **Carbohydrates:** 18g
- **Fiber:** 6g
- **Sugar:** 4g

Cooking Tips

- If you want to make the soup richer, you can use low-fat coconut milk instead of almond milk.
- For extra flavor, roast the cauliflower before adding it to the pot.
- If the soup is too thick for your liking, add more almond milk or vegetable broth to thin it out.

Health Benefits

- Cauliflower is high in fiber and low in calories, making it a great option for digestive health. It's also packed with antioxidants that support the immune system.
- Almond milk keeps the soup creamy without adding dairy, making it easier to digest for those with sensitivities or digestive concerns.
- This soup is light yet filling, perfect for a soothing, nutritious lunch or dinner.

Butternut Squash Soup with Coconut Milk

- **Time of Preparation:** 10 minutes
- **Cooking Time:** 30 minutes
- **Serving Units:** 4 servings

Ingredients

- 1 medium butternut squash, peeled and cubed
- 1 small onion, chopped
- 2 garlic cloves, minced
- 2 cups low-sodium vegetable broth
- 1 cup light coconut milk
- 1 tablespoon olive oil
- 1/2 teaspoon ground ginger
- Salt and pepper to taste
- Fresh cilantro for garnish (optional)

Procedure

- In a big saucepan, warm up the olive oil over medium heat. Add the garlic and onion and sauté until aromatic and tender.
- Stir in the cubed butternut squash, ginger, and vegetable broth. Once the squash is soft, lower heat and simmer for 20 to 25 minutes after bringing to a boil.
- Add the coconut milk and blend the soup using an immersion blender until smooth.
- Season with salt and pepper to taste. Garnish with fresh cilantro before serving.

Nutritional Values (Per Serving)

Calories: 190

Protein: 3g

Fat: 9g

Carbohydrates: 25g

Fiber: 6g

Sugar: 7g

Cooking Tips

- If you want a deeper flavor, roast the butternut squash in the oven at 400°F

(200°C) for about 20 minutes before adding it to the soup.
- For added texture, serve with a sprinkle of toasted pumpkin seeds on top.
- Adjust the creaminess by using more or less coconut milk depending on your preference.

Health Benefits

- Butternut squash is rich in beta-carotene and vitamins A and C, which support immune function and skin health. It's also high in fiber, aiding digestion.
- Coconut milk adds healthy fats and a subtle sweetness to the soup without overwhelming the dish with dairy.
- This soup is both satisfying and soothing, making it a great option for an evening meal that's easy on the digestive system.

These easy, soothing soups offer the perfect combination of comfort and nutrition, making them ideal for individuals seeking to nourish their body while managing pancreatitis. Each recipe features ingredients known for their anti-inflammatory and digestive benefits, ensuring that you can enjoy delicious meals that are gentle on the stomach. Whether you're in the mood for a vibrant carrot and ginger puree or a creamy cauliflower soup, these recipes will leave you feeling satisfied and rejuvenated.

7

Fiber-Rich Dinners for Digestive Support

Fiber-rich dinners are essential for maintaining digestive health, particularly for those managing conditions like pancreatitis. In addition to helping with digestion, fiber also helps control blood sugar and maintains intestinal health. Not only does it support smoother digestion, but it also contributes to overall wellness by keeping cholesterol levels in check and preventing blood sugar spikes. Incorporating fiber into your evening meals can help you feel full and satisfied, reducing the urge to overeat or snack late at night. The following recipes focus on fiber-packed ingredients like lentils, quinoa, vegetables, and whole grains to create satisfying, nutritious dinners that are gentle on the stomach while providing plenty of flavor and variety. These meals are also rich in essential nutrients, ensuring that while you care for your digestive health, you are also nourishing your body with vitamins, minerals, and antioxidants. By choosing these balanced, fiber-forward meals, you can enjoy a variety of delicious dishes that support your overall health and well-being.

Lentil and Spinach Stew

- **Time of Preparation:** 10 minutes
- **Cooking Time:** 30 minutes
- **Serving Units:** 4 servings

Ingredients

- 1 cup dried green or brown lentils, rinsed
- 1 small onion, chopped
- 2 carrots, peeled and diced
- 2 garlic cloves, minced
- 4 cups low-sodium vegetable broth
- 1 teaspoon cumin
- 1 teaspoon paprika
- 4 cups fresh spinach leaves
- 1 tablespoon olive oil
- Salt and pepper to taste
- Fresh parsley for garnish (optional)

Procedure

- In a big saucepan, warm up the olive oil over medium heat. Add the onion, garlic, and carrots, and sauté for 5-7 minutes until softened.
- Stir in the cumin and paprika, cooking for another minute to release their flavors.
- Add the lentils and vegetable broth. Bring to a boil, then reduce the heat to low and simmer for 25 minutes, or until the lentils are tender.
- Stir in the fresh spinach and cook for an additional 2-3 minutes until the spinach wilts.
- If preferred, sprinkle with fresh parsley and season with salt and pepper to taste.

Nutritional Values (Per Serving)

- **Calories:** 260
- **Protein:** 15g
- **Fat:** 5g
- **Carbohydrates:** 42g
- **Fiber:** 15g
- **Sugar:** 6g

Cooking Tips

- If you prefer a thicker stew, mash some of the lentils with the back of a spoon before serving.

- For added flavor, squeeze in some fresh lemon juice right before serving.
- Store leftovers in an airtight container in the fridge for up to 3 days—this stew reheats beautifully!

Health Benefits

- Lentils are packed with fiber and plant-based protein, helping to keep you full and promoting healthy digestion. They are also rich in folate and iron, essential for energy and immune function.
- Spinach is high in antioxidants, vitamins A and C, and provides a hefty dose of fiber and essential minerals like magnesium.
- This stew is nutrient-dense and low in fat, making it a great option for anyone seeking a hearty, fiber-rich dinner that supports digestive health.

Quinoa and Broccoli Stir-Fry

- **Time of Preparation:** 10 minutes
- **Cooking Time:** 20 minutes
- **Serving Units:** 2 servings

Ingredients

- 1 cup quinoa, rinsed
- Two cups of water or vegetable broth low in sodium
- 1 small head of broccoli, cut into florets
- 1 bell pepper, sliced
- 1 small carrot, julienned
- 2 tablespoons olive oil
- 2 tablespoons low-sodium soy sauce or tamari (for gluten-free)
- 1 teaspoon sesame oil (optional)
- 1 tablespoon sesame seeds (optional, for garnish)

Procedure

- Bring the vegetable broth or water to a boil in a medium-sized saucepan. Add the quinoa, reduce the heat to low, cover, and simmer for 15 minutes until the quinoa is tender and the liquid is absorbed. Using a fork, fluff and set aside.
- In the meantime, warm up some olive oil in a big pan over medium heat. Add the broccoli, bell pepper, and carrot, and sauté for 5-7 minutes until the vegetables are tender but still crisp.
- Stir in the cooked quinoa and soy sauce, cooking for another 2 minutes until everything is heated through.
- Drizzle with sesame oil if desired, and sprinkle with sesame seeds for added crunch.
- Serve hot and enjoy!

Nutritional Values (Per Serving)

- **Calories:** 380
- **Protein:** 12g
- **Fat:** 16g
- **Carbohydrates:** 48g
- **Fiber:** 8g
- **Sugar:** 4g

Cooking Tips

- Feel free to switch up the vegetables based on what you have on hand—

zucchini, snap peas, or mushrooms would work well here.
- You can prepare the quinoa in advance and store it in the fridge, cutting down on cooking time during busy weeknights.
- For a spicy kick, add a sprinkle of red pepper flakes or a dash of sriracha.

Health Benefits

- Quinoa is a complete protein and a good source of fiber, making it ideal for digestion and energy maintenance. It's also gluten-free and packed with essential amino acids.
- Broccoli is rich in fiber, vitamins C and K, and folate, which all contribute to digestive and overall health.
- This stir-fry is a filling, plant-forward meal that is low in fat, high in nutrients, and easy to digest.

Baked Eggplant with Tomato and Feta

- **Time of Preparation:** 10 minutes
- **Cooking Time:** 35 minutes
- **Serving Units:** 2 servings

Ingredients

- 1 large eggplant, sliced into rounds
- 2 tablespoons olive oil
- 1/2 cup low-sodium canned diced tomatoes
- 1/4 cup crumbled feta cheese
- 1 teaspoon dried oregano
- Salt and pepper to taste
- Fresh basil leaves for garnish (optional)

Procedure

- Preheat the oven to 375°F (190°C). Line a baking sheet with parchment paper.
- Add salt and pepper to the eggplant slices after brushing them with olive oil on both sides. Place them on the baking sheet that has been prepared in a single layer.
- Bake for 25-30 minutes, turning halfway through, until the eggplant is tender and golden.
- Remove the eggplant from the oven and spoon the diced tomatoes over the slices. Sprinkle with feta cheese and oregano.
- Return the tray to the oven and bake for another 5-7 minutes, until the cheese is slightly melted and the tomatoes are heated through.
- Add some fresh basil leaves as a garnish and serve.

Nutritional Values (Per Serving)

- **Calories:** 220
- **Protein:** 6g
- **Fat:** 14g
- **Carbohydrates:** 20g
- **Fiber:** 7g
- **Sugar:** 9g

Cooking Tips

- For extra flavor, grill the eggplant slices on an outdoor grill or grill pan instead of baking them.

- If you're not a fan of feta, you can substitute it with a sprinkle of nutritional yeast for a dairy-free, cheesy flavor.
- Serve with a side of brown rice or a green salad to make this a more substantial meal.

Health Benefits

- Eggplant is a low-calorie, fiber-rich vegetable that supports heart health and digestion. Its spongy texture allows it to absorb flavors beautifully.
- Feta cheese provides a tangy contrast to the eggplant and is lower in fat compared to many other cheeses, offering a great way to enjoy dairy in moderation.
- This dish is light, flavorful, and packed with fiber, making it ideal for a healthy dinner that's both filling and easy on the stomach.

Brown Rice with Steamed Greens and Tofu

- **Time of Preparation:** 10 minutes
- **Cooking Time:** 25 minutes
- **Serving Units:** 2 servings

Ingredients

- 1 cup brown rice
- Two cups of water or vegetable broth low in sodium
- 1 block (200g) firm tofu, cubed
- 1 bunch kale or spinach, stems removed and leaves chopped
- 2 tablespoons soy sauce or tamari (for gluten-free)
- 1 tablespoon olive oil
- One teaspoon of sesame oil (for taste only, optional)
- Salt and pepper to taste
- Sesame seeds for garnish (optional)

Procedure

- In a medium pot, bring water or broth to a boil. Add the brown rice, reduce heat to low, cover, and simmer for 20-25 minutes until the rice is tender and the liquid is absorbed.
- While the rice is cooking, heat olive oil in a skillet over medium heat. Add the cubed tofu and cook for 5-7 minutes, turning occasionally, until golden brown on all sides.
- Steam the kale or spinach in a steamer basket over a pot of boiling water for 3-5 minutes, until just wilted.
- Once the rice is cooked, fluff it with a fork and stir in the steamed greens and tofu. Season to taste with salt and pepper and drizzle with soy sauce and sesame oil, if using.
- Serve warm, garnished with sesame seeds if desired.

Nutritional Values (Per Serving)

Calories: 420

Protein: 18g

Fat: 14g

Carbohydrates: 54g

Fiber: 8g

Sugar: 2g

Cooking Tips

- To add more flavor to the tofu, marinate it in a mixture of soy sauce, garlic, and ginger for 15 minutes before cooking.
- If you prefer a crunchier texture, press the tofu for 15-20 minutes to remove excess moisture before cooking.
- For extra nutrition, consider adding other steamed veggies like carrots or bell peppers to this dish.

Health Benefits

- Brown rice is a whole grain high in fiber, which supports digestive health and helps keep blood sugar levels stable.
- Tofu is an excellent source of plant-based protein and calcium, and it's easy to digest, making it a great protein option for those managing pancreatitis.
- Steamed greens like kale and spinach are packed with vitamins A, C, and K, as well as fiber, helping to reduce inflammation and support gut health.

These fiber-rich dinners are not only packed with essential nutrients but are also easy to prepare and gentle on the digestive system. By incorporating plant-based proteins, whole grains, and an abundance of vegetables, these recipes provide filling, nutritious meals that are perfect for supporting digestive health. Whether you're enjoying a hearty lentil stew or a simple quinoa stir-fry, each dish offers a balance of flavor and nutrition that's sure to leave you feeling satisfied and nourished.

8

Comforting Desserts and Treats

When it comes to desserts and treats, indulging in something sweet doesn't have to be unhealthy. These comforting, low-fat, and nutrient-packed desserts are perfect for individuals managing pancreatitis or anyone looking for gentle, satisfying treats. Using whole ingredients like fruits, oats, and coconut, these recipes are not only delicious but also offer digestive support and energy. Each dessert provides a balance of natural sweetness, healthy fats, and fiber to satisfy your cravings without compromising your health. Additionally, these recipes are designed to be simple and easy to prepare, using minimal processed ingredients to keep them as wholesome as possible. Whether you're looking for a quick snack or a light dessert after a meal, you'll find these options both nourishing and flavorful, making it easy to enjoy something sweet while staying mindful of your wellness.

Baked Pears with Cinnamon

- **Time of Preparation:** 5 minutes
- **Cooking Time:** 30 minutes
- **Serving Units:** 2 servings

Ingredients

- 2 ripe pears, halved and cored
- 1 teaspoon ground cinnamon
- 1 teaspoon honey or maple syrup (optional)
- 1/2 teaspoon vanilla extract
- 1/4 cup water

Procedure

- Preheat the oven to 350°F (175°C). Place the pear halves, cut side up, in a small baking dish.
- Drizzle the honey or maple syrup (if using) over the pears, and sprinkle with cinnamon and vanilla extract. Pour the water into the bottom of the baking dish to prevent the pears from drying out.
- Bake for 25-30 minutes, or until the pears are soft and slightly caramelized.
- Serve warm, optionally topped with a spoonful of low-fat yogurt or a sprinkle of chopped nuts.

Nutritional Values (Per Serving)

- **Calories:** 120
- **Protein:** 0g
- **Fat:** 0g
- **Carbohydrates:** 30g
- **Fiber:** 6g
- **Sugar:** 18g

Cooking Tips

- Make sure to use ripe pears for the best sweetness and texture.
- For a more decadent dessert, serve the baked pears with a dollop of Greek yogurt or a scoop of dairy-free coconut ice cream.
- Feel free to experiment with additional spices like nutmeg or ginger to complement the cinnamon.

Health Benefits

- Pears are rich in dietary fiber, which helps promote digestive health and

regularity. They also provide natural sweetness, making them perfect for a light dessert.
- Cinnamon offers anti-inflammatory properties and can help regulate blood sugar levels, making it a great addition to any dessert.
- This simple, comforting treat is low in fat and packed with nutrients, making it a great option for a guilt-free dessert.

Banana and Oat Cookies

- **Time of Preparation:** 10 minutes
- **Cooking Time:** 15 minutes
- **Serving Units:** 12 cookies

Ingredients

- 2 ripe bananas, mashed
- 1 1/2 cups rolled oats
- 1/4 cup unsweetened applesauce
- 1 teaspoon vanilla extract
- 1/2 teaspoon ground cinnamon
- 1/4 cup raisins or chopped nuts (optional)

Procedure

- Preheat the oven to 350°F (175°C). Line a baking sheet with parchment paper.
- Mash the bananas till smooth in a big basin. Stir in the oats, applesauce, vanilla extract, and cinnamon until well combined. Add chopped nuts or raisins, if using.
- Place dough in tablespoon-sized quantities onto the baking sheet that has been prepared, gently pressing them down with the back of the spoon.
- Bake for 12-15 minutes, or until the cookies are golden and firm to the touch.
- Before serving, allow the cookies to cool for a few minutes.

Nutritional Values (Per Cookie)

- **Calories:** 70
- **Protein:** 1g
- **Fat:** 1g
- **Carbohydrates:** 15g
- **Fiber:** 2g
- **Sugar:** 5g

Cooking Tips

- To get the finest flavor and natural sweetness, use extremely ripe bananas.
- You can add other mix-ins like dried cranberries, chocolate chips (if tolerated), or coconut flakes to change up the flavor.
- Store leftover cookies in an airtight container for up to 3 days, or freeze them for longer storage.

Health Benefits

- Bananas are an excellent source of potassium, which supports heart and muscle function, and they also provide natural sweetness and fiber.
- Oats are high in soluble fiber, which helps stabilize blood sugar levels and supports digestive health.
- These cookies are a healthy, low-fat alternative to traditional treats, offering sweetness without the guilt.

Coconut Rice Pudding

- **Time of Preparation:** 5 minutes
- **Cooking Time:** 25 minutes
- **Serving Units:** 4 servings

Ingredients

- 1/2 cup short-grain rice (such as Arborio or sushi rice)
- 1 1/2 cups light coconut milk
- 1 cup water
- 2 tablespoons honey or maple syrup
- 1 teaspoon vanilla extract
- Ground cinnamon for garnish (optional)

Procedure

- Rice, water, and coconut milk should all be combined in a medium pot. Bring to a boil over medium heat, then reduce the heat to low and simmer, stirring occasionally, for 20-25 minutes until the rice is soft and the mixture has thickened.
- Stir in the honey or maple syrup and vanilla extract, and cook for an additional 2-3 minutes until well combined.
- Before serving, remove from the heat and allow it cool slightly. If preferred, garnish with a dusting of ground cinnamon.

Nutritional Values (Per Serving)

- **Calories:** 180
- **Protein:** 3g
- **Fat:** 4g
- **Carbohydrates:** 33g
- **Fiber:** 1g
- **Sugar:** 9g

Cooking Tips

- Stir the rice frequently to prevent it from sticking to the bottom of the pot and ensure a creamy texture.
- For added flavor, you can top the pudding with fresh fruit like mango, pineapple, or berries.
- If you prefer a thicker pudding, simmer for a few extra minutes until the desired consistency is reached.

Health Benefits

- Coconut milk provides healthy fats and a creamy texture without the need for dairy, making this dessert easier on the digestive system.
- Rice is a gentle source of carbohydrates that's easy to digest, making it a great option for individuals managing pancreatitis or other digestive concerns.
- This rice pudding is naturally sweetened with honey or maple syrup, offering a comforting treat without refined sugars.

Apple and Berry Compote

- **Time of Preparation:** 5 minutes
- **Cooking Time:** 15 minutes
- **Serving Units:** 4 servings

Ingredients

- Diced, peeled, and cored two medium apples
- 1 cup mixed berries (fresh or frozen)
- 1 tablespoon honey or maple syrup
- 1/2 teaspoon ground cinnamon
- 1/4 cup water
- 1 teaspoon lemon juice (optional)

Procedure

- In a medium saucepan, combine the diced apples, berries, honey, cinnamon, and water. Over medium heat, bring to a simmer, stirring periodically.
- Reduce the heat to low and cook for 10-15 minutes, until the fruit is soft and the mixture has thickened. Stir in the lemon juice if desired for a bit of brightness.
- Before serving, take the compote off the fire and let it cool a little. Serve warm or chilled, on its own or with a spoonful of yogurt or oatmeal.

Nutritional Values (Per Serving)

- **Calories:** 100
- **Protein:** 1g
- **Fat:** 0g
- **Carbohydrates:** 25g
- **Fiber:** 4g
- **Sugar:** 18g

Cooking Tips

- If using frozen berries, there's no need to thaw them beforehand—just add them straight to the saucepan.
- For extra richness, you can stir in a tablespoon of almond butter or sprinkle some nuts on top before serving.
- This compote keeps well in the fridge for up to 5 days and can be enjoyed as a topping for pancakes, toast, or even ice cream.

Health Benefits

- Apples and berries are both high in fiber and antioxidants, which promote gut health and reduce inflammation.
- This compote is naturally sweetened with honey or maple syrup, avoiding refined sugars while still delivering a deliciously sweet flavor.
- It's a light, fruit-based dessert that can be enjoyed on its own or as a topping for yogurt, oatmeal, or other dishes.

These comforting desserts and treats are designed to satisfy your sweet tooth without compromising your digestive health. Each recipe is packed with natural ingredients, offering a balance of sweetness, fiber, and nutrients that are gentle on the stomach. Whether you're baking pears with cinnamon or whipping up a batch of banana and oat cookies, these recipes provide a healthy, indulgent way to end your meal or enjoy a snack.

9

7-Day Meal Plan for Lasting Pancreatic Health

Managing pancreatic health through diet can be both rewarding and delicious. This 7-day meal plan is designed to offer balanced, nutrient-rich meals that are easy on the digestive system while providing the variety and flavors you crave. With carefully crafted recipes for breakfast, lunch, snacks, and dinner, this guide will help you stay on track with your health goals while enjoying tasty and satisfying meals each day.

Day-by-Day Breakfast Guide

A healthy breakfast sets the tone for the day, fueling you with the energy you need while being gentle on the pancreas. Each breakfast in this meal plan is packed with fiber, protein, and healthy fats to keep you satisfied and support lasting pancreatic health.

Day 1: Creamy Oatmeal with Stewed Apples
Warm oats with cinnamon and tender apples make for a hearty, gut-friendly start to the day. The soluble fiber in oats helps stabilize blood sugar, while apples provide vitamins and fiber that promote digestive health.
Day 2: Fluffy Egg White Scramble with Spinach
A simple scramble of egg whites and spinach delivers protein and iron without overloading the digestive system. This low-fat meal is ideal for those managing pancreatitis, providing energy without unnecessary fat.
Day 3: Banana Chia Pudding
Prep this chia pudding the night before for an easy grab-and-go breakfast. Packed with fiber and omega-3s, chia seeds help reduce inflammation and keep you feeling full throughout the morning.
Day 4: Gut-Soothing Smoothie Bowl
Blend frozen bananas, spinach, and almond milk for a refreshing smoothie bowl topped with fresh berries and a sprinkle of chia seeds. This breakfast is light yet nutrient-dense, providing antioxidants and fiber.
Day 5: Greek Yogurt with Blueberries and Honey
Creamy Greek yogurt paired with antioxidant-rich blueberries and a drizzle of honey offers a protein-packed breakfast that's also gentle on your digestive system.
Day 6: Avocado Toast on Whole Grain Bread
Top whole grain toast with mashed avocado, a sprinkle of lemon juice, and fresh herbs. The healthy fats in avocado and fiber in the bread make this a filling and nutrient-rich breakfast.
Day 7: Quinoa Porridge with Berries
Swap oats for quinoa to boost your protein intake while still enjoying a warm, comforting porridge. Add fresh berries for a burst of flavor and antioxidants to support pancreatic health.

Day-by-Day Lunch Guide

Lunch should be nourishing, light, and satisfying to keep you energized for the rest of the day. Each lunch is packed with fiber, lean protein, and anti-inflammatory ingredients to support your digestive health while being easy to prepare.

Day 1: Quinoa Salad with Cucumber and Avocado
A refreshing salad made with quinoa, crunchy cucumber, and creamy avocado. This plant-based, fiber-rich meal is both filling and packed with healthy fats to keep you full and energized.
Day 2: Chicken and Sweet Potato Lettuce Wraps
Lean chicken and roasted sweet potatoes wrapped in crisp lettuce provide a light but

satisfying lunch. Low in fat and high in fiber, this meal is easy on the pancreas and full of flavor.	Sliced apples baked with cinnamon make for a sweet, fiber-rich snack that's easy on digestion and packed with antioxidants.
Day 3: Lentil and Vegetable Soup	**Day 2:** Rice Cakes with Avocado Spread
A warm, hearty lentil soup with plenty of vegetables like carrots, celery, and spinach. Lentils are a great source of plant-based protein and fiber, making this soup a comforting and nutritious midday meal.	Whole grain rice cakes topped with creamy avocado and a sprinkle of lemon juice. This snack is both crunchy and satisfying, with plenty of healthy fats to keep you full.
Day 4: Grilled Zucchini and Hummus Wrap	**Day 3:** Greek Yogurt with Blueberries
Grilled zucchini slices wrapped in a whole grain tortilla with creamy hummus and fresh veggies make for a simple, portable lunch that's light but nutrient-packed.	A simple snack of low-fat Greek yogurt topped with fresh blueberries. Rich in protein and antioxidants, this snack supports digestive health and keeps you satisfied.
Day 5: Brown Rice and Steamed Greens with Tofu	**Day 4:** Cucumber and Carrot Sticks with Yogurt Dip
A bowl of fiber-rich brown rice, tender steamed greens, and crispy tofu drizzled with a light soy sauce dressing. This plant-forward meal supports digestive health and provides lasting energy.	Crisp cucumber and carrot sticks paired with a light, tangy yogurt dip make for a refreshing, low-calorie snack that's easy to prepare.
Day 6: Poached Chicken Breast with Steamed Veggies	**Day 5:** Banana and Oat Cookies
A classic, lean lunch of poached chicken breast served with steamed broccoli and carrots. Low in fat and high in protein, this meal is easy to digest and full of essential nutrients.	These naturally sweet cookies made with bananas and oats offer a healthy way to satisfy your sweet tooth while providing fiber and slow-release energy.
	Day 6: Hummus with Bell Pepper Slices
Day 7: Quinoa and Broccoli Stir-Fry	Creamy hummus served with fresh bell pepper slices. This fiber-packed snack is rich in plant-based protein and perfect for mid-afternoon munching.
Quinoa and broccoli stir-fried with a splash of olive oil and soy sauce. This quick and healthy dish is rich in fiber, antioxidants, and plant-based protein.	**Day 7:** Pear with a Sprinkle of Cinnamon
	A simple yet satisfying snack of sliced pear topped with a sprinkle of cinnamon. This low-fat, high-fiber snack supports digestive health and helps curb sugar cravings.

Day-by-Day Snack Guide

Snacks play an important role in keeping your energy levels steady throughout the day. These snack ideas are packed with fiber, healthy fats, and natural sweetness to curb hunger without spiking blood sugar or straining the pancreas.

Day 1: Baked Apple Slices with Cinnamon

Day-by-Day Dinner Guide

End your day with a nutrient-dense dinner that supports digestion, provides fiber, and helps your body repair overnight. These dinners are hearty, delicious, and easy on the pancreas, making them perfect for maintaining lasting pancreatic health.

Day 1: Lentil and Spinach Stew
A warm and filling stew made with lentils, fresh spinach, and aromatic spices like cumin and paprika. This fiber-rich dish is satisfying and easy to digest, perfect for a soothing dinner.
Day 2: Baked Eggplant with Tomato and Feta
Sliced eggplant baked with juicy tomatoes and crumbled feta cheese. This Mediterranean-inspired dish is low in fat and full of flavor, providing plenty of fiber and antioxidants.
Day 3: Grilled Salmon with Quinoa and Asparagus
A lean, protein-packed dinner of grilled salmon served with fluffy quinoa and tender asparagus. Salmon's omega-3 fatty acids support heart and pancreatic health, while quinoa adds fiber and essential nutrients.
Day 4: Brown Rice with Steamed Greens and Tofu
A simple yet nourishing dinner of brown rice, steamed kale or spinach, and crispy tofu. This plant-based meal is packed with fiber, vitamins, and protein to keep you full and support digestion.
Day 5: Butternut Squash Soup with Coconut Milk
A creamy, comforting soup made with butternut squash and light coconut milk. Full of vitamins A and C, this soup is naturally sweet and easy to digest, perfect for a cozy dinner.
Day 6: Poached Cod with Lemon and Herbs
A light, protein-packed dinner of poached cod seasoned with lemon and fresh herbs, served with steamed vegetables. This low-fat meal is gentle on the digestive system and full of flavor.
Day 7: Quinoa-Stuffed Bell Peppers
Bell peppers stuffed with quinoa, vegetables, and a sprinkle of cheese. These fiber-rich peppers are satisfying and packed with vitamins, making them the perfect way to end the week.

This 7-day meal plan is designed to make maintaining pancreatic health both enjoyable and sustainable. Each meal is crafted to provide a balance of fiber, protein, healthy fats, and essential nutrients, all while being gentle on the digestive system. By following this meal plan, you'll nourish your body with the nutrients it needs to support long-term pancreatic health and overall well-being.

Conclusion

As you reach the final pages of this "Pancreatitis Diet Cookbook 2025", it's important to reflect on the journey you've embarked on and the strides you've made toward better health. Managing pancreatitis through diet may seem overwhelming at first, but as you've discovered, it's a path that is not only achievable but can also be filled with delicious, nourishing, and satisfying meals. Every meal you prepare is a step toward feeling better, gaining strength, and taking control of your wellness journey.

The recipes and nutritional guidelines provided in this book were created with your well-being in mind, ensuring that you have the tools to support your digestive health while also enjoying a diverse range of flavors. By following these principles, you're doing more than just feeding your body; you're fostering an environment for healing and long-term wellness. Every meal you prepare is a step toward regaining control, reducing flare-ups, and maintaining a life of comfort and vitality.

It's crucial to remember that the process of managing pancreatitis is not just about eliminating harmful foods—it's about embracing a new lifestyle of mindful eating. With each dish, you're choosing ingredients that support your pancreas, stabilize your energy levels, and promote better digestion. Whether you're creating a soothing breakfast, a hearty lunch, or a comforting dinner, the recipes in this book are meant to ease your daily routine and bring joy back into cooking and eating.

You've also learned that eating for pancreatitis doesn't mean sacrificing flavor or variety. Through these pages, you've discovered how to turn nutrient-dense, low-fat foods into meals that are vibrant, flavorful, and easy to prepare. This balance of health and enjoyment is key to staying consistent in your dietary habits, and it's what will help you sustain this lifestyle for the long term.

While pancreatitis may present challenges, this cookbook is a reminder that those challenges can be met with practical solutions. Cooking can once again become a source of comfort and creativity, not just an obligation. You've already taken the essential steps by learning to prepare meals that are gentle on your pancreas while being full of taste and nutrition.

As you continue your journey beyond these pages, remember that progress takes time. Every meal is an opportunity to support your body's healing, and consistency is what will make the biggest difference in the long run. Be patient with yourself, celebrate your victories—both big and small—and know that you're building a foundation for long-term health.

This is not just a diet; it's a lifestyle change that can empower you to live fully and without fear of flare-ups. With the right knowledge and meal plan, you're equipped to thrive. Keep exploring new ingredients, refining your cooking techniques, and most importantly, listening to your body's needs.

In the end, the kitchen becomes a place of healing, and food transforms into a source of both nourishment and pleasure. We hope this cookbook has made the process of managing pancreatitis more approachable and has inspired you to cook with confidence, knowing that each meal brings you closer to better health.

Here's to your ongoing journey of healing, wellness, and the joy of eating! Let these recipes be your guide as you continue to live well, thrive, and enjoy every bite along the way.

Printed in Dunstable, United Kingdom

66208801R00054